HORSE POWER

SPARKY'S STEM GUIDE TO

TRUCKS

BY KIRSTY HOLMES

KidHaven
PUBLISHING

Published in 2023 by **KidHaven Publishing,
an Imprint of Greenhaven Publishing, LLC**
29 East 21st Street
New York, NY 10010

Edited by: Emilie Dufresne
Designed by: Danielle Rippengill

Cataloging-in-Publication Data

Names: Holmes, Kirsty.
Title: Sparky's STEM guide to trucks / Kirsty Holmes.
Description: New York : KidHaven Publishing, 2023. |
Series: Horse power | Includes glossary and index.
Identifiers: ISBN 9781534540453 (pbk.) | ISBN 9781534540477
(library bound) | ISBN 9781534540460
(6 pack) | ISBN 9781534540484 (ebook)
Subjects: LCSH: Trucks--Juvenile literature.
Classification: LCC TL230.15 H635 2023 |
DDC 629.224--dc23

Printed in the United States of America

CPSIA compliance information: Batch #CSKH23: For further information contact Greenhaven Publishing
LLC, New York, New York at 1-844-317-7404.

Please visit our website, www.greenhavenpublishing.com. For a free
color catalog of all our high-quality books, call toll free 1-844-317-7404
or fax 1-844-317-7405.

IMAGE CREDITS

CONTENTS

WORDS THAT LOOK LIKE <u>this</u> CAN BE FOUND IN THE GLOSSARY ON PAGE 24.

WELCOME TO DRIVING SCHOOL!

HELLO! I'm Jeremy Sparkplug, world-famous truck driver. You can call me Sparky. You must be the new recruits. Welcome to the Horses for Courses School of Motoring!

Here you will be learning about some of the biggest and toughest **vehicles** on wheels: trucks! If you pass your driving test, you'll earn your Golden Horseshoe. So pay attention: it's time to DRIVE!

What You Need to Know

How big the WHEELS are! ☐

What LOADS trucks can carry! ☐

Where do you SLEEP? ☐

Whose TEDDY BEAR is this? ☐

LESSON 1:
WHAT IS A TRUCK?

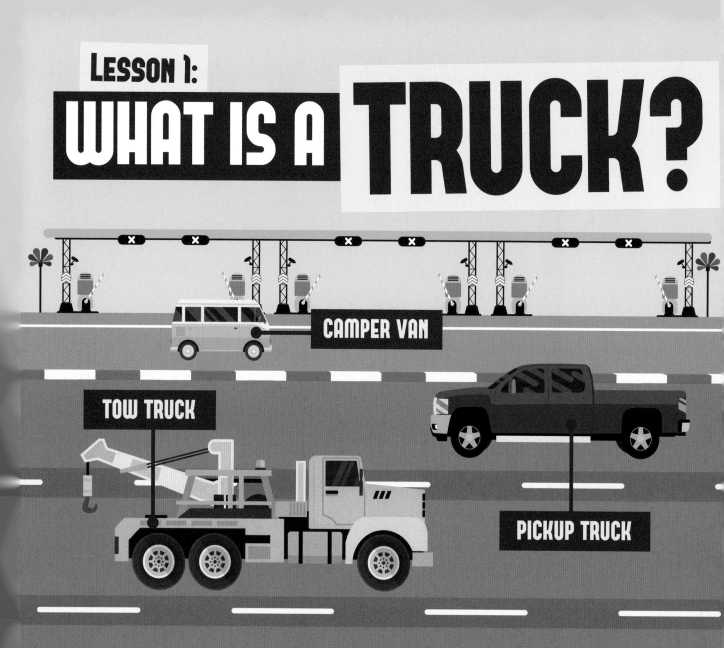

CAMPER VAN

TOW TRUCK

PICKUP TRUCK

A truck is a type of vehicle used for carrying things. Trucks can carry many different things, both small and very large. Trucks drive on roads, and come in lots of different types and sizes.

LESSON 2:
PARTS OF A TRUCK

CARGO

Cargo means the load the truck is carrying. This is usually at the back of the truck.

Let's look at the parts of a truck.

WHEELS

Trucks can have very large wheels – up to several feet across!

8

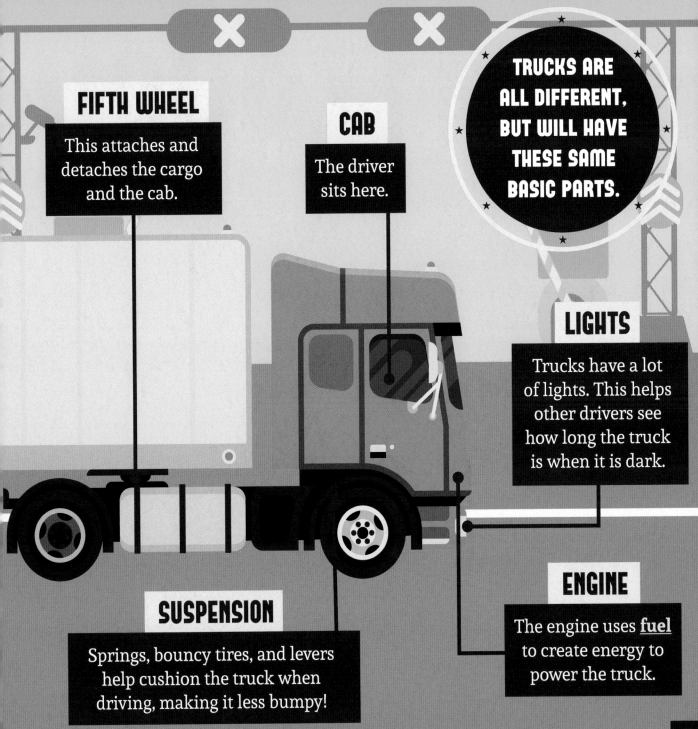

FIFTH WHEEL

This attaches and detaches the cargo and the cab.

CAB

The driver sits here.

TRUCKS ARE ALL DIFFERENT, BUT WILL HAVE THESE SAME BASIC PARTS.

LIGHTS

Trucks have a lot of lights. This helps other drivers see how long the truck is when it is dark.

SUSPENSION

Springs, bouncy tires, and levers help cushion the truck when driving, making it less bumpy!

ENGINE

The engine uses **fuel** to create energy to power the truck.

INSIDE A TRUCK

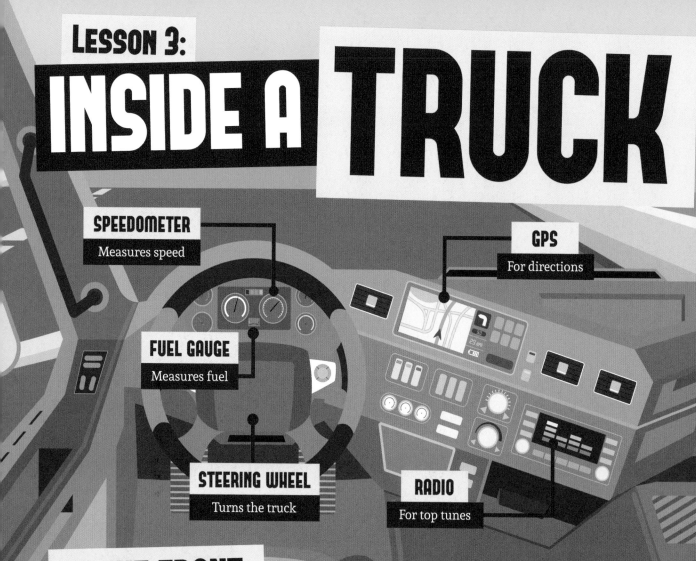

SPEEDOMETER
Measures speed

GPS
For directions

FUEL GAUGE
Measures fuel

STEERING WHEEL
Turns the truck

RADIO
For top tunes

IN THE FRONT

Let's take a look inside the cab of Peggy's sleeper truck.
This truck is for driving long distances, so she has to sleep

IN THE BACK

The back of the cab has a little living area for Peggy.
It has everything she needs for nights on the road.

BED

FRIDGE

CLOTHES

LET'S HIT THE
ROAD

TEDDY BEAR

FLASHLIGHT

TV

LOADS!

Trucks can carry lots of different things.

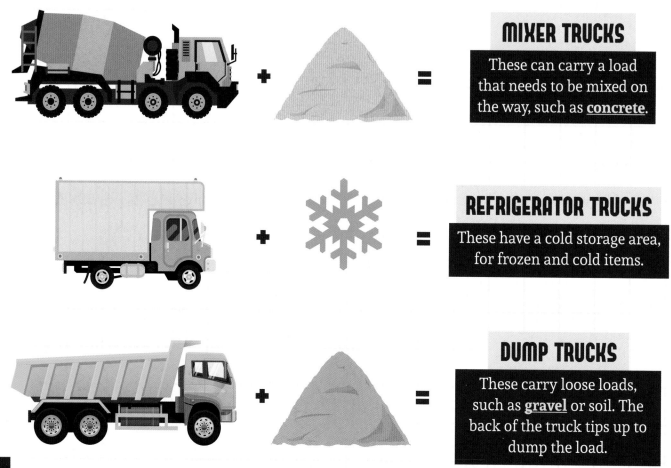

MIXER TRUCKS

These can carry a load that needs to be mixed on the way, such as **concrete**.

REFRIGERATOR TRUCKS

These have a cold storage area, for frozen and cold items.

DUMP TRUCKS

These carry loose loads, such as **gravel** or soil. The back of the truck tips up to dump the load.

Each truck has a different shape and size to be able to do its job.

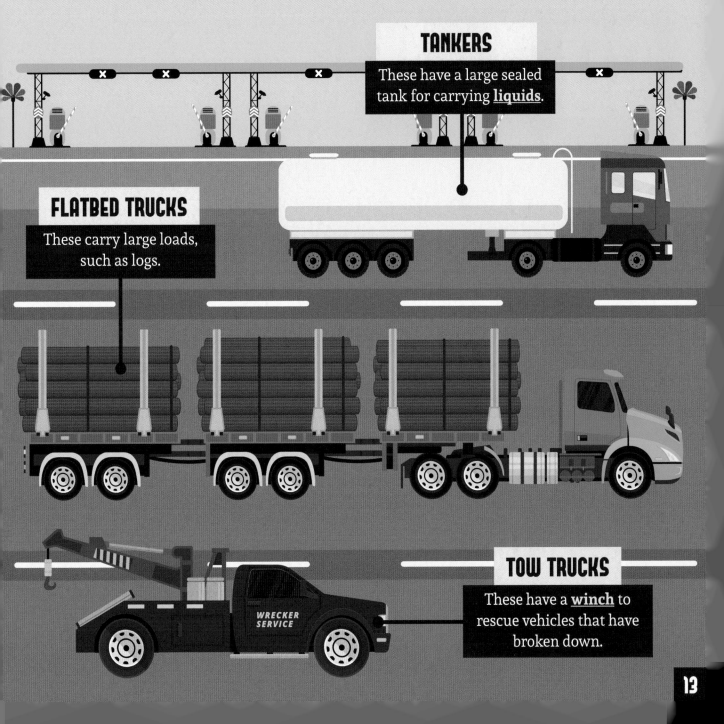

TANKERS
These have a large sealed tank for carrying **liquids**.

FLATBED TRUCKS
These carry large loads, such as logs.

WRECKER SERVICE

TOW TRUCKS
These have a **winch** to rescue vehicles that have broken down.

SAFETY!

Trucks can be enormous, so it's important that anyone driving a truck, especially on **public** roads, knows how to stay safe.

Take it from a truck driver like me: ALWAYS do your safety checks.

SAFETY FEATURES

NO PHONES

Drivers should always concentrate on the road and not get distracted.

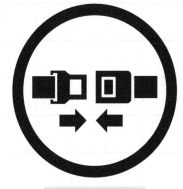

SEAT BELT

A strap holds you in your seat in case there is a crash.

LIGHTS

Lights help other drivers see the truck at night.

SPEED LIMITERS

Special computers in the engine can stop a truck from going too fast.

SAFETY SIGNS

Getting too close to a big truck can be dangerous.

TAKING BREAKS

Drivers should not drive for more than nine hours in a day.

LESSON 6:
THE TITAN

One of the world's biggest trucks is the Terex 33-19 "Titan."

The Terex 33-19 "Titan" was built to work at an iron mine and could carry a load weighing 360 tons (326 tonnes). Its huge tires were over 10 feet (3 m) across. Only one of these trucks was ever made.

The "Titan" weighs around 500 tons (450 tonnes)!

LESSON 7:
TERRIFIC TRUCKS

SHEEP GAS

The gases produced by a single sheep in one day could be enough to power a small truck for 25 miles (40 km)!

$1,000,000

MOST EXPENSIVE TRUCK

The Sultan of Johor in Malaysia had a **custom-built** Mack Super-Liner made so he could tow his speedboat.

LONGEST ROAD TRAIN EVER

In **deserted** areas, long trucks with many trailers attached can form a road train. The longest ever was the Mack Titan in Australia. It had 113 trailers and was over 0.86 mile (1.4 km) long!

HOGS

ICE ROAD TRUCKERS

In the coldest parts of the world, lakes and rivers freeze so hard that truckers can drive on them – but only if they are brave and skillful. These drivers take cargo to hard-to-reach places during the winter.

DRIVING TEST

Woah there, learners. Time to giddy-up over to the test and see if you're a top trucker – or whether you've just been "foaling" around! (Check your answers on page 21!)

Questions

1. Which part of a truck does the driver sleep in?

2. What is the GPS for?

3. What type of cargo do tankers carry?

4. What is the maximum time you can drive a truck in one day?

5. What color was the Terex 33-19 "Titan"?

Did you get them all right?

Answers: 1. In the back of the cab 2. Directions 3. Liquids 4. 9 hours 5. Green

Of course you did – here is your Golden Horseshoe.
You are now a tip-top trucker, just like me and Peggy!

MONSTER TRUCK MADNESS

Monster truck drivers crash around and perform crowd-pleasing feats of craziness! It takes years of training. But we're professionals, so let us show you how it's done...

STEP ONE
Get BIG wheels

STEP TWO
Get a crowd

STEP THREE
Get muddy

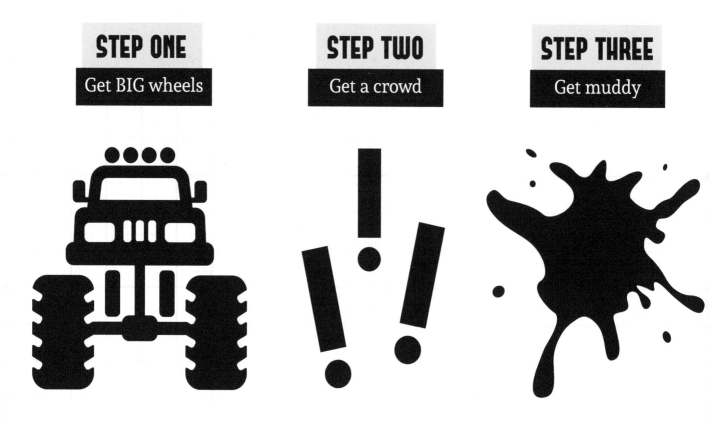

GLOSSARY

CONCRETE   a man-made material that is a bit like stone, used for building

CUSTOM-BUILT   built specially for one person, exactly how they want it

DESERTED   not having many buildings or people

FUEL   a material used to make heat or power

GRAVEL   small stones and pebbles

LIQUIDS   materials that flow, such as water

PUBLIC   not private; open to people in the area

VEHICLES   machines for carrying or transporting things or people

WINCH   a machine that uses ropes to pull things

INDEX